Large Print
Colour & Frame

———————————————

Mindfulness

31 relaxing colouring
pages to enjoy

Published by Richardson Publishing Limited.
www.richardsonpublishing.com

10 9 8 7 6 5 4 3 2 1

© 2023 Richardson Publishing Limited.

All illustrations and typesetting by Clarity Media Ltd.

Cover design by Hannah Wadham.

ISBN 978-1-913602-39-0

Printed and bound by Bell & Bain Ltd, 303 Burnfield Road, Thornliebank, Glasgow G46 7UQ.

A catalogue record for this book is available from the British Library.

If you would like to comment on any aspect of this book, please contact us at:

E-mail: puzzles@richardsonpublishing.com

Follow us and @ us to share your artwork!

🐦 @puzzlesandgames
📷 @richardsonpuzzlesandgames
📘 @richardsonpuzzlesandgames
▶️ @richardsonpuzzlesandgames
♪ @richardsonpuzzlesngames